Yellowing Photographs

Yellowing Photographs

Poems by

Shelby Lynn Lanaro

© 2021 Shelby Lynn Lanaro. All rights reserved.
This material may not be reproduced in any form, published,
reprinted, recorded, performed, broadcast,
rewritten or redistributed without
the explicit permission of Shelby Lynn Lanaro.
All such actions are strictly prohibited by law.

Cover design by Shay Culligan

ISBN: 978-1-954353-62-6

Kelsay Books
502 South 1040 East, A-119
American Fork, Utah, 84003
Kelsaybooks.com

To Charlie, my love.
May the sidewalk continue to fill with our yellowing photographs.

Acknowledgments

Many thanks to the following places that first homed versions of some of the poems in this collection:

Better Than Starbucks: "Peeling Potatoes with My Mother at the Kitchen Sink," "Trying Not to Cry at Starbucks"

Dying Dahlia Review: "God as Woman"

The Feminist Wire: "Flowers, I thought"

Gnashing Teeth: "Reimagining Olives"

Poetry Breakfast: "Sidewalk Talk"

Stormy Island Publishing: "Restless Reticence"

Verse of Silence: "Apartment by the Train Station," "Operation Downfall"

The Wild Word: "Date Night," "Yellowing"

Young Ravens Literary Review: "Life Quickly Steeps," "To the Woman"

Contents

Yellowing	11
Fermented Moment	12
Operation Downfall	13
Negative Cutting	14
To My Beloved Percy	15
Flowers, I thought	17
God as Woman	18
My Mother's Hairbrush	19
Peeling Potatoes with My Mother at the Kitchen Sink	21
Apartment by the Train Station	22
Restless Reticence	23
Shifting Gears	24
Reimagining Olives	25
Karma	27
Trying Not to Cry at Starbucks	28
Lunacy	29
Date Night	30
Breakfast at Your Father's	31
Sidewalk Talk	32
To the Woman	33
Life Quickly Steeps	35

Yellowing

A glass of lemonade on a summer
Sunday, when I was a child,
and school seemed so September

away. Sunlight streaked for hours
after I finished my supper,
so I skipped rope in the driveway,

splashed through the sprinkler
Daddy made of the hose,
spritzing water into sky.

But rain falls on yellow days,
colors fade to gray. Summers
become just more days

of the work week, and hop-scotch
outlines are yellowing photographs
on the sidewalk.

Fermented Moment

Smocked in one of Daddy's old
T-shirts to spare my clothes
of stains, I stood in the bed

of his red, Nissan hardbody
burrowing my hands
in bundles of grapes, freshly

picked off the vine
in Nana and Papa's backyard.
Purple painted my palms

as the bushels made their way
down an assembly line
of my aunts, uncles, and cousins

to Papa, who packed
the fermented fruit
with guttural grinds

of the wine press. Juice-soaked
wood saturated the musk of the garage.
As a child, I couldn't taste the sweet

fruit of my family's labor
through the bitterness
of watered-down alcohol,

and since we stopped making wine
when Papa died,
I never will.

Operation Downfall

You never let me open
your old suitcase
from the war. *It's too
fragile,* you'd always say,

and I'd romanticize
its unknown contents.
I've pictured letters,
yellowed photographs

signed with Nana's
lipstick and longing.
Maybe some memorabilia,
souvenirs (if you can

call them that) you picked up
while occupying Okinawa.
Or maybe a farewell
handkerchief, embroidered

with your initials
and your mother's fear.
But maybe all that remains
in this tattered suitcase

is grayed memories best
forgotten.
And now that you're gone,
I can't bring myself

to open it;
my expectations
of its contents
are too fragile.

Negative Cutting

My memories are an old-timey movie.
A haze lingers over them—a yellowed film
reeling over my life. Some things

I wish I could recover: the sound
of my grandfather's voice,
the distinct rasp of him singing

with his guitar that now sits
in my bedroom in the same condition
he left it twenty-some-odd years ago.

I wish I could recapture going
fishing, and campfires, collecting
eggs with him from the chicken coop,

but then there are too many things I wish
I could forget, so I cut those negatives out
trying to resplice the rest.

To My Beloved Percy

My dear, it has taken me two years
to write this. Forgive me, but I couldn't
find words enough to pay you proper tribute,
though I think I've found them now;

they were buried in the odd places
where you used to dig: the couch,
your bed, my bed, the carpet. I breathe
in your scent that still lingers on the deep

pink neck pillow you stole from me.
It was striking against your fawn fur.
How could I have said no?
Everything that was my favorite

was your favorite, too, because if it was
yours and it was mine, then we were together.
I press my forehead against our pillow
as if to say *sorry* for letting you go

too long in pain. Do you remember
how I used to sing softly to you at night?
I was there to hear your borning cry.
I wasn't, of course, but you were with me

for fifteen years. I was there when you
were old and calm enough to let me
put my face to yours—your grayed, black
velvet face. I'm sorry I didn't sing to you

that final day, which shouldn't have caught me
so off guard. If I were dramatic, I'd tell you
this: I went back to work that day—not
because I didn't care, but because my heart

could have stopped beating, too,
if I'd have let it. Know that your food bowl
still sits in its place waiting for you
to pick it up and gently toss it

to let me know you are hungry. Your soul
still nourishes mine, so I wanted to write
for you the perfect poem.
I hope this will do.

Flowers, I thought

would brighten up the room,
so a pot of yellow daisies sits
on the windowsill leaning
to the left, sometimes the right.
Each day is different.

And each day I move the pot
turning it until the daisies lean
in toward the kitchen.
Until yesterday

when I realized the daisies
don't turn left or right.

They turn to the sun
knowing they don't belong
indoors.
They try to escape
the confines of my kitchen,
perhaps hoping

I'll do the same.

God as Woman

Trust in God—she will provide.
    —Emmeline Pankhurst

In kindergarten, I pictured
God for the first time
and He was a woman.

Not because I'm a woman,
and not because
I'm a feminist.

Growing up in church,
we prayed the "Our *Father*,"
and I still do.

But being raised by a single
mother, who brought me
to church every week,

who taught me
The Commandments
in Sunday School,

and, when I was older,
led my youth group
and confirmation classes,

of course I picture God
as a woman.

My Mother's Hairbrush

It would hurt, and I'd try
not to cry
as my mother's hairbrush raked

against my scalp.
There were hundreds
of bristles, hard and sharp,

and she'd brush my long hair
until my tears were the only
things worse than my matted snarls.

*Stop crying, or I'll give you
something to cry about*

she'd say—the reaction of a long,
hard workday at a job that was never
meant to be a forty-plus year career.

A single mother, she'd come home
to cook, clean,
watch the Disney Channel (again),

give her daughter a shower,
brush out the day's snarls,
and send her off to bed.

I don't know what she'd do
after I'd gone to sleep,
but I often wonder

if she'd wished—if she still
wishes—she'd had someone
to talk to. To cry to.

Now, in my twenties, I pour
two glasses of wine, watch
Downton Abbey (again),

and try my hardest
to brush out
my mother's snarls.

Peeling Potatoes with My Mother at the Kitchen Sink

We stood for five minutes—
ten minutes? More?

We could have spoken,
sped up the time. Could have

gossiped about church,
about my brother's impulsive

marriage that neither of us
agreed with, but we didn't.

We peeled potatoes in silence,
for however long it took,

concentrating on peeling back
wet skin from fleshy

pieces of boiled potato—
our fingers pruning

from the pot of water.
I thought of my grandmother;

she must have taught my mom
to cook her potatoes

before peeling.
It makes it so much easier

she said before we'd started,
then nothing.

Apartment by the Train Station

In your twenties, it's depressingly
romantic—living

on the second floor
of a stranger's house,

sharing rent with someone
you hardly know.

Where the rattle of the midnight
train splits silky night

like the lover
rapping on your bedroom window

so he doesn't wake your roommate
(he'll have to sneak back into darkness

before the 5:00 a.m. whistle blows
and she stumbles in sleepy

stupor to the bathroom)
solely because it's exciting to keep

intimacies tied
to the timing of train tracks.

Restless Reticence

By the bayside, we sat
on a blanket of sassy
lilac. The sun dripped
down the horizon
like spun honey,

and we watched water
pearl on our sand-dusted
feet. Your bare arm
grazed mine—an alabaster
chill in jalapeño heat.

My heart blushed rave
red while any words
we wished we could have
said swept up in ebb tide.

Shifting Gears

Buzzed off Bud Light, I leaned
back in the passenger seat
of your old, black GTI.

The Roots rang out the windows,
and the air smelled cool—autumn's
salute to winter. The moon was high

and so were we. My eyes closed,
but *the music played on, and told me
I was meant to be awake,* meant to be

there, with you, gazing through the moon
roof at the stars as you just drove
like we always did when we were

in college and had nowhere else
to go. That night, though, you took
my hand in yours between gear

shifts. Sobriety surged through
my goosebumps, and I watched,
warily, as the embers from your

Marb Reds blazed
on my jacket. Then, one by one,
they burned out.

Reimagining Olives

We were broke when we first moved
in together, got by on clipping
coupons. We watched *Chopped* enough

to know how to repurpose
groceries: salvage components of last night's
dinner and reimagine them

into tomorrow's lunch.
Today I learned to tapenade
with yesterday's black olives. Next week

I'll attempt to stir-fry
the leftovers I'll take
from eating with my mother

at home.

I still call her house *home*
even though I haven't lived there
in almost three years.

My bedroom of two and a half decades
is now a guest room,
but I'm no guest.

I'll still go in, close the door behind me
when I need a break. I still lie
on the sun-faded, purple carpet

that soaked up my teenage tears
from boys who came and went. I'll finger
the spot that took a burning

from a forgotten flatiron, tear up thinking
I neglected a foundation
that always embraced me. And while I now

have you, with all my free time spent busy
budgeting and reimagining my food
to make it more interesting,

I guess I haven't quite yet reimagined home.

Karma

I stole a Buddha once
from Quincy Market

when the vendor
wasn't looking.

It was one-inch-tall
and only cost one dollar,

but there were three of us:
my two best friends and me.

That's three Buddhas
and three dollars.

We had never stolen. None of us
were even Buddhists.

Ten years later, I found
my Buddha. A cross

and my guilt had stuffed it
in the back of a drawer.

One day I'll go back
to Quincy Market,

leave a few dollars on a cart
that sells religious icons.

For now, I'll pray
an Our Father, ask forgiveness,

and hope The Buddha
leads me to Enlightenment.

Trying Not to Cry at Starbucks

You tell me all the things you crave
in this life: the velvet of your voice
smoothing over a crowd like hot tea
on a sore throat; you want to dabble

in different facets of entertainment.
You're not just a singer, you say,
you want to be an actor, on Broadway,
sing opera, be a rock star.

I try to keep up and pump caramel,
chocolate sauce, vanilla, and raspberry
into my coffee—which one of these things
doesn't belong? It seems we

always have our deepest conversations
over lattes and cappuccinos—
a quiet coffee shop's bull crashing into
customers' concentration.

I try not to cry over my chai
as I wonder if, after spending six
years together, you value your career
more than me. Then I marvel in how many

patrons must be salivating
over our conflicting views of how far
one should let the boundaries of passion
spill into his personal life. Our rapport,

as of now, is an overfilled mug; coffee
stains the outside in streaks,
puddles onto the unwashed table, and joins
the burn of others' spilled-over romances.

Lunacy

We hate nature but love the stars.
Remember the time we pulled off
the road somewhere in the desert
and made love beneath the moon?

Did I imagine it?

How we love to love each other's
bodies by the light of the night
sky. Remember that Christmas
you bought glow-in-the-dark

stars for our bedroom? We created
our own constellations that night
but never did put up the moon.
We didn't want to compromise

our tides. You don't like the harvest
best like me, but we can still love
each other; the ceiling separates
the moon from our lunacy.

Date Night

The colors of evening floated
like lily pads on the still water.
We didn't think about going back
to America, to stressful
schoolwork, soulless job

searching. We just sat, smiled,
the two of us, at a tiny table
outside a café on the Limmat
River as downtown Zurich
glowed in lamplight.

I refuse to kiss you when you smoke
at home, but something about Europe,
about your Swiss roots,
made me think you looked sexy
that night perching a Chesterfield

between index and middle fingers,
leaning back in your chair
elbow propped on the arm. No cares,
no worries about work, school,
finding a career; that was a career—

drinking cappuccino and smoking
a cigarette at ten o'clock
on a Wednesday night.
You always said
the Swiss do it right.

Breakfast at Your Father's

We had just walked
Oberrohrdorf's cobblestone
streets to the village center

to get fresh-baked bread
for breakfast. Light
as challah, warm as the bed

we had shared into
late mornings.
I sat at the patio table

eating spoonfuls of hazelnut
yogurt, savoring creamy bites
with bits of nuts.

You'd brought out the bread
to me, handed over butter.
You talked with your father

about home and work
as I watched clouds linger
over the Alps, mourning

that we couldn't stay
in that warm, challah bed
because New England

would greet us with haste
over breakfast (if we're lucky):
black coffee and dry toast at the office.

Sidewalk Talk

What are your dreams?
you ask me puffing peach-mint
hookah smoke outside
the falafel house on Howe.

*Where do you want to go
in the world?
What will be your legacy?*

I'm not sure how to answer,
but I know the night is calm.
The air moves freely, not pushed
by wind, and the stars don't feel

need to outshine streetlamps.
They're content behind the curtain
of clouds, yet still shining; they know
they are, know their purpose.

And I'm content, sitting here,
not yet knowing mine.

To the Woman

I.

To the woman in the stall
next to me: I've been you.
Being broken-hearted
in a public bathroom
is like a rite of passage.
Somehow, we find solace
in our little sanctuaries,
foster silent relationships
with strangers
through our stifled sobs.
Know that I want to
ask you if you're doing
all right. But I don't
want to pry. Please
take this toilet paper tissue
as a token—a peace
offering—and realize
that I have been there too.

II.

To the woman in the stall
next to me: I know you
think you've been me.
I know you think I'm broken-
hearted. And I am. But not
how you've been. I've been
sitting still in this stall
for an hour now, and when

I move, the automated
valve will flush out
my miscarriage.
My phone says the pain
should subside quickly
if it's complete, but pain
is relative and so is time.
And in time, I know
I'll have to leave
this sanctuary,
say my goodbyes.
I reach for your hand,
take the makeshift tissue
you've offered me.
Please know I can't
bring myself to choke out
a *thank you,*
but thank you just the same.

Life Quickly Steeps

When we make a cup of tea,
we run off
to do something—anything—else

besides wait
as the timer ticks. How rarely
we watch as herbs flavor water.

Mint, rose hips, elderberry
marry steaming liquid,
while the water eases the release

of herbal essences, pouring
from their paper sachet; a dear
friend spilling its soul.

As the timer ticks to its final beep,
we make a choice:

1) we deem ourselves too impatient
to wait for the infusing to finish,
cut its time short, wring the bag,
and throw it away;

2) we allow the immersion
its full duration. Remain
in restraint for the timer to end.

Whether in haste or in reverence,
we still drink up life's nectar; or

3) we forget the timer and our tea.
Let it over-steep in careless abandon.
Neglect always leaves
a bitter taste on the tongue.

About the Author

Shelby Lynn Lanaro is a poet and professor. In 2017, Shelby received her MFA from Southern Connecticut State University, where she now teaches First Year Composition and Creative Writing. A New England native, Shelby and her husband, Charlie, live in a log cabin in the woods of Connecticut. Along with writing, Shelby enjoys cooking and photography. Several of her photographs have appeared in *Young Ravens Literary Review.*

www.ingramcontent.com/pod-product-compliance
Lightning Source LLC
Chambersburg PA
CBHW071642090426
42738CB00013B/3189